THEY CALL ME WOOLLY

What Animal Names Can Tell Us

Keith DuQuette

G. P. Putnam's Sons

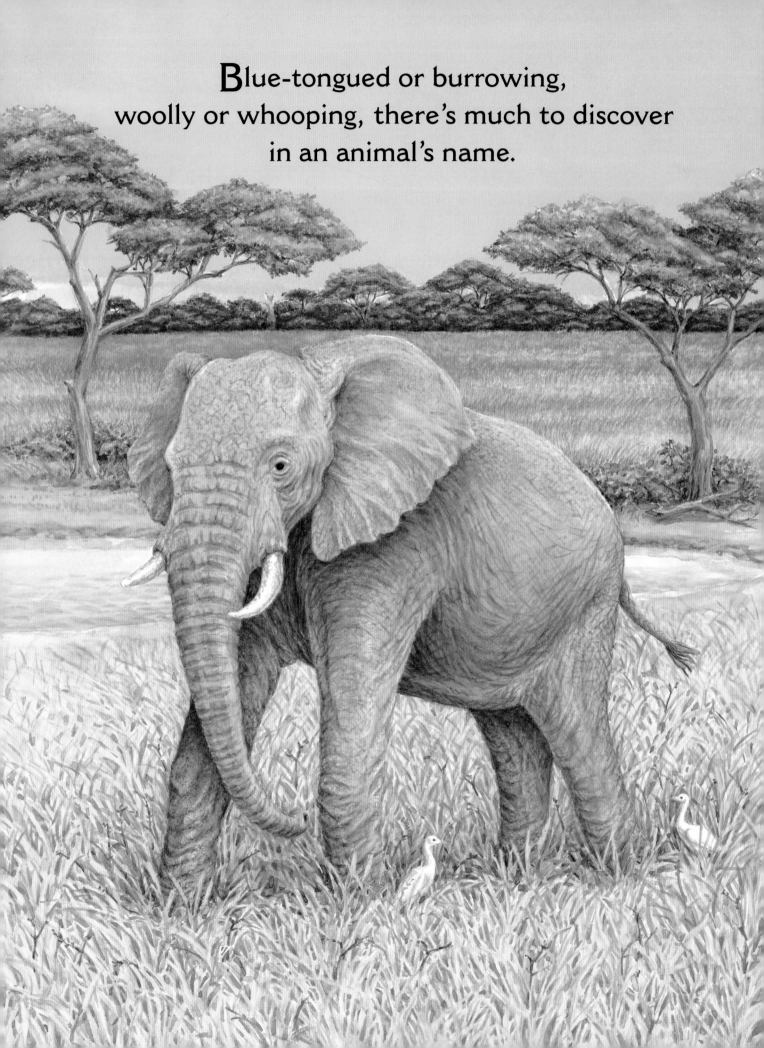

Blue-tongued or burrowing,
woolly or whooping, there's much to discover
in an animal's name.

A name can tell you
where an animal is from:
the **African elephant**
and the **American alligator**.

Or it can tell you
about the animal's habitat:
the **polar bear**
and the **mountain goat**.

Or where it often roosts and nests:
the **barn owl**
and the **chimney swift**.

Some animals are named
for how they move around:
the **grasshopper**, the **burrowing owl**
and the **roadrunner**.

Other animals are named
for their calls:
the **howler monkey**
and the **whooping crane**.

Or the sounds they make
with their wings or tails:
the **hummingbird**
and the **rattlesnake**.

Still others are named
for the food they eat:
the **rat snake**
and the **bee-eater**.

The **white shark**,
the **blue marlin** and the **yellow goatfish**
are named for their color.

Some animals are named
for their fur or skin:
the **woolly monkey**
and the **thorny devil**.

Animals can be named for their unique features:
the **hammerhead shark**, the **long-eared bat**,
the **blue-tongued skink** and the **spoonbill**.

The **zebra butterfly**, the **leopard frog**
and the **tiger salamander**
are named for other animals
with spots or stripes like theirs.

Some animals look just like their names:
the **walkingstick** and the **thornbug**.

While others look nothing like
what you might expect:
the **tarantula hawk** and the **woolly bear**.

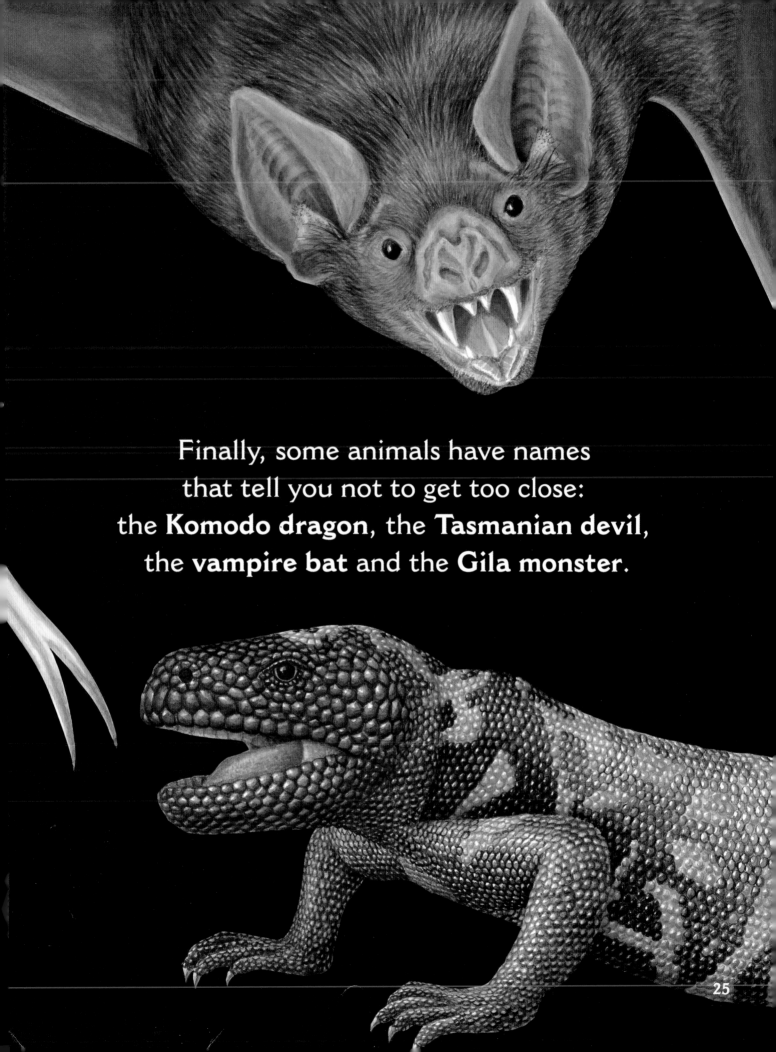

Finally, some animals have names
that tell you not to get too close:
the **Komodo dragon**, the **Tasmanian devil**,
the **vampire bat** and the **Gila monster**.

Here are some interesting facts about the animals in this book:

AFRICAN ELEPHANT

(page 2) The largest living land mammal, the African elephant can weigh up to 14,000 pounds. It can eat over 400 pounds of plant material a day. It stands 10 to 13 feet at the shoulders, is up to 25 feet long, including the trunk, and is found in sub-Saharan Africa. There are two species of elephant, African and Asian.

AMERICAN ALLIGATOR

(page 3) It will eat almost any animal that dares to swim, walk or fly into its territory. This is the largest reptile in North America, ranging in length from 7 to 15 feet. It is found in the rivers and swampy lowlands of the southeastern United States. There are two species of alligator, American and Chinese.

BARN OWL (page 6)

Found throughout much of the world, barn owls only come out at night and are rarely seen. Barn owls can hunt in total darkness, finding their prey by sound. They stand 14 to 20 inches tall and have a wingspan of over 3 feet.

BEE-EATER (page 13)

This bright-colored bird skillfully captures bees and wasps in midair. It rubs its captured prey against branches or the ground before eating it, presumably to destroy the stinger. It stands 6 to 14 inches from head to tail and is found throughout Africa, Europe, Asia and Australia.

BLUE MARLIN (page 15)

This giant billfish is one of the world's fastest swimmers, achieving speeds of over 40 miles per hour. It reaches lengths of over 12 feet, weighs up to 1,400 pounds and is found in warm and tropical seas throughout the world.

BLUE-TONGUED SKINK

(page 19) When threatened, this slow-moving Australian lizard displays its long blue tongue, probably to surprise its enemies. It reaches lengths of 14 to 22 inches.

BURROWING OWL (page 8)

This ground-dwelling bird usually lives in abandoned prairie dog burrows. However, it can dig its own hole with its claws and beak. It stands up to 9 inches tall and is found in deserts and prairies throughout the Western Hemisphere.

CHIMNEY SWIFT (page 7)

A fast-flying bird, the chimney swift builds its nest of twig fragments glued together with saliva, attaching them to the inside of unused chimneys or hollow trees. This 5-inch-long bird is sometimes referred to as a "cigar with wings." It breeds in North America and spends winters in South America.

GILA MONSTER (page 25)
This lizard, named for the Gila River Basin in Arizona, is one of only two poisonous lizards. Its bites are painful but rarely fatal to humans. It grows up to 20 inches in length and is found in the southwestern United States and northern Mexico.

GRASSHOPPER (page 8)
This insect is well known for its long leaps and familiar summer songs. It varies in size from less than ½ inch up to 4 inches long. It is found in tropical and temperate regions throughout the world.

HAMMERHEAD SHARK (page 18) It is thought that this shark's uniquely flattened, wide head may serve as a rudder, making it a more efficient swimmer. Some species reach lengths of 15 feet. They are found in warm and temperate oceans throughout the world.

HOWLER MONKEY (page 10) It is one of the loudest animals on earth. Its territorial howl, which sounds like a dog's bark, can be heard as far as 2 miles away. One of the largest of the New World monkeys, its head and body reach 36 inches in length, with a 36-inch-long tail. It is found in the forests of South and Central America.

HUMMINGBIRD (page 11)
There are over 300 species of these "flying jewels." In some species their rapidly beating wings (as many as 80 times a second) produce the humming sound for which they are named. They vary in length from 2 to 8 inches and are found throughout North and South America.

KOMODO DRAGON (page 24) Named for Komodo Island in Indonesia, where it is found, this largest living lizard grows up to 10 feet in length and weighs as much as 300 pounds. It is a strong and fearsome predator, attacking wild pigs, deer and even people!

LEOPARD FROG (page 20)
If disturbed on land, this meadow frog quickly leaps away in a series of zigzagging jumps, seeking refuge in the water. It can jump as far as 6 feet, over 15 times its body length! It is 2 to 5 inches long and is found in the United States and Canada.

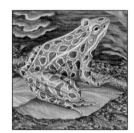

LONG-EARED BAT (page 18)
This bat's exceptionally long ears are an essential part of its hunting equipment—they are used to listen to the movements of their insect prey. This bat is 3 to 6 inches from head to tail and has a wingspan of 9 to 11 inches. It is found in Europe and Asia and has related species in North America.

MOUNTAIN GOAT
(page 5) This sure-footed climber is found on the rugged mountain peaks of the western United States and Canada. Its skid-resistant hooves have a sharp, hard rim enclosing a soft inner pad that enables it to climb narrow ledges and steep, icy slopes. It stands 40 inches tall, grows up to 65 inches long and weighs as much as 300 pounds.

POLAR BEAR (page 4)
This large inhabitant of the Arctic is an excellent swimmer and can remain underwater for as long as 2 minutes in search of food. On land, it is surprisingly fast and can outrun a caribou over a short distance. It grows as tall as 5 feet, as long as 8 feet and ranges in weight from 900 to 1,500 pounds.

RAT SNAKE (page 12)
This large, nonpoisonous snake climbs trees and enters buildings in search of rodents and other small prey, including chickens. For this reason it is sometimes called the "chicken snake." It reaches lengths of 3 to 8 feet and is found in North America, Europe and Asia.

RATTLESNAKE (page 11)
This well-known venomous snake's rattle is made up of segmented rings at the end of the tail. These rings make a buzzing noise when shaken, apparently to warn other animals to stay away. Rattlesnakes reach lengths of up to 8 feet and are found in North and South America.

ROADRUNNER (page 9)
A member of the cuckoo family, the roadrunner is a weak flyer because of its short wings. It can run as fast as 15 miles per hour, skillfully dodging predators or chasing prey. It measures 20 to 24 inches in length and is found in the southwestern United States and Mexico.

SPOONBILL (page 19)
When feeding, this large wading bird sweeps its bill from side to side, snapping it shut on small fish, shrimp and insects, all of which it detects by touch. It ranges in height from 24 to 35 inches and is found in warm regions throughout the world.

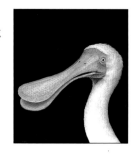

TARANTULA HAWK (page 23) This is actually a large wasp. The female delivers a paralyzing sting to a tarantula. She then lays her eggs on the tarantula, and when they hatch, they feed on the live tarantula. They grow over 2 inches long, including the leg span, and are found in the southwestern United States.

TASMANIAN DEVIL (page 24) Named for the island of Tasmania, south of Australia, where it is found, this raccoon-size marsupial devours its prey with its powerful jaws, including the bones! Its head and body are 21 to 30 inches long, with a 9- to 12-inch bushy tail.

THORNBUG (page 22)
This insect spends its life clinging to the stems of saplings, piercing the bark and sucking up sap. Its remarkable resemblance to a large rose thorn camouflages it from predators. It measures up to ½ inch long and is found in the American tropics.

THORNY DEVIL (page 17)
The unique thornlike spines of this lizard have two functions, protection and providing drinking water. Overnight, dew collects on the thorns, and water trickles along tiny grooves in the skin to the thorny devil's mouth. It is found in the deserts of Australia and can grow 6 to 8 inches in length.

TIGER SALAMANDER (page 21) The largest land-dwelling salamander, it grows from 6 to 14 inches in length. The adult lives under logs or in animal burrows. It comes out at night, especially after heavy rains, in search of worms and bugs, and is found throughout North America.

VAMPIRE BAT (page 25)
This bat feeds exclusively on blood, mainly that of cattle and horses, often attacking the same animal night after night. It measures up to 3½ inches in length with a wingspan up to 8 inches and is found in Central and South America.

WALKINGSTICK (page 22)
There are about 2,000 species of this plant-feeding insect found in tropical and temperate regions throughout the world. Also known as stick insects, their uncanny resemblance to twigs or leaves makes them one of nature's best-camouflaged creatures. One species reaches lengths of 12 inches.

WHITE SHARK (page 14)
Also known as the great white shark, this tireless predator cruises the oceans in search of prey. It feeds on fish, seals and dolphins and has been known to attack people! It has reached record lengths of 21 feet and weights of 7,000 pounds. It is found in warm and temperate oceans around the world.

WHOOPING CRANE
(page 10) One of the world's rarest birds, its trumpetlike whooping call can be heard several miles away. It is the tallest American bird, standing up to 5 feet, with a wingspan of over 7 feet. It breeds in Canada and spends winters in the United States.

WOOLLY BEAR (page 23)
This bristly caterpillar matures into the tiger moth. It is black on both ends and brownish red in the middle. According to superstition, the amount of black in the caterpillar's coating forecasts the severity of the coming winter—the more black showing, the worse the winter. It grows to over 2 inches long and is found throughout North America.

WOOLLY MONKEY
(page 16) This peaceful, agile monkey lives in the upper levels of mountain forests, rarely ever coming down to the forest floor. Its dense, woolly coat makes it well adapted to this moist, chilly habitat. Its head and body measure 20 to 26 inches and tail 23 to 28 inches in length. It is found near the Amazon basin of South America.

YELLOW GOATFISH
(page 15) One of over 50 species of goatfish found in tropical and temperate seas worldwide, it has two whiskerlike sensory chin barbels, which are used for finding food. These barbels are said to resemble a goat's beard. The goatfish reaches lengths of 15 inches.

ZEBRA BUTTERFLY
(page 20) The caterpillar of this butterfly feeds on poisonous passion flower vines and passes the substance on to the mature butterfly. Its striking yellow and black markings warn predators away. It has a wingspan of over 3 inches and is found in the wooded areas of the American South.

Here are some more revealing animal names to explore:

ARCHERFISH
This small fish shoots a stream of water at insects resting on plants above the water. This causes the insects to fall into the water where the fish can eat them.

CATBIRD
The catbird is not a cat, but a woodland bird named for its catlike mewing call.

CHICKEN TURTLE
Native Americans and early settlers to the American South ate this turtle. It is said to taste just like chicken.

COOKIE-CUTTER SHARK
This small predatory shark is named for the perfectly oval shape of its bite.

FIDDLER CRAB
The male crab of this species has one claw much bigger than the other and often holds the claws so that it looks as if it's playing a fiddle.

GLASS LIZARD
This snakelike lizard is known for its brittle tail. When attacked, its tail shatters into several pieces, helping the lizard escape. Later, the tail grows back.

HAPPYFACE SPIDER
The unique markings on this Hawaiian spider look like a grinning, cartoonish face.

HONEYPOT ANT
Some of the workers of this semidesert ant store nectar and water within their swollen abdomens. They feed the rest of the colony during the long dry season.

LOVEBIRD
This little parrot forms a strong bond with its mate. Pairs are often seen perched close together.

SOAPFISH
When threatened, this warm-water fish's skin releases a soapy, foaming slime that is mildly poisonous.

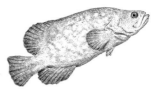

POCKET MOUSE
This small burrowing rodent is named for its fur-lined external cheek pouches, where it stores its food.

STARGAZER
This bottom-dwelling fish is known for the eyes on top of its head, always pointing toward the sky.

POISON-DART FROG
This bright-colored frog is one of the most poisonous animals in the world. Tribesmen of South and Central America spread the poison on the tips of blowgun darts.

STINKPOT
When disturbed, this freshwater American turtle releases a foul-smelling yellowish fluid. It's also known as the "stinking jim."

RIGHT WHALE
Sailors gave this slow-swimming whale its name because it was rich in oil and bone, was easy to kill and floated when dead. It was the "right" whale to catch.

SUNGAZER
This African lizard can be seen basking in the morning sun with its head pointed sky-ward.

SECRETARY BIRD
The crest of quills on this large African bird's head was said to resemble the long quill pens that secretaries from preindustrial times tucked into their wigs.

TRAPDOOR SPIDER
A close relative of the tarantula, it builds a silk-lined burrow with a hinged lid where it launches attacks on passing insects.

to Virginia

G. P. PUTNAM'S SONS,
a division of Penguin Putnam Books for Young Readers,
345 Hudson Street, New York, NY 10014.
G. P. Putnam's Sons, Reg. U.S. Pat. & Tm. Off.
Published simultaneously in Canada.
Printed in Hong Kong by South China Printing Co. (1988) Ltd.
Designed by Sharon Murray Jacobs.
Text set in twenty-one point Cantoria.
The art was done in watercolor, gouache and colored pencil.
Library of Congress Cataloging-in-Publication Data
DuQuette, Keith.
They call me Woolly : what animal names can tell us / Keith DuQuette.
p. cm. 1. Zoology—Nomenclature (Popular)—Juvenile literature.
[1. Animals. 2. Vocabulary.] I. Title.
QL355 .D8 2002 590—dc21 00-055356
ISBN 0-399-23445-4
1 3 5 7 9 10 8 6 4 2
FIRST IMPRESSION